Neil Champion..........

Heinemann
LIBRARY

**www.heinemann.co.uk**

Visit our website to find out more information about **Heinemann Library** books.

To order:
☎ Phone 44 (0) 1865 888066
🖹 Send a fax to 44 (0) 1865 314091
🖳 Visit the Heinemann Bookshop at www.heinemann.co.uk to browse our catalogue and order online.

First published in Great Britain by Heinemann Library, Halley Court, Jordan Hill, Oxford OX2 8EJ, a division of Reed Educational and Professional Publishing Ltd.

Heinemann is a registered trademark of Reed Educational & Professional Publishing Limited.

OXFORD  MELBOURNE  AUCKLAND
JOHANNESBURG  BLANTYRE  GABORONE
IBADAN  PORTSMOUTH NH (USA)  CHICAGO

© Reed Educational and Professional Publishing Ltd 2000

Designed by Celia Floyd
Illustrations by Jeff Edwards
Originated by HBM Print Ltd, Singapore
Printed in Hong Kong by Wing King Tong

ISBN 0 431 03672 1 (hardback)
04 03 02 01 00
10 9 8 7 6 5 4 3 2 1

ISBN 0 431 03681 0 (paperback)
04 03 02 01 00
10 9 8 7 6 5 4 3 2 1

**British Library Cataloguing in Publication Data**

Champion, Neil
    Rock climbing. – (Radical sports)
    1. Rock climbing – Juvenile literature
    I. Title
    796.5'223

**Acknowledgements**

The Publishers would like to thank the following for permission to reproduce photographs:

Mountain Camera, pp. 4, 6-24, 28 (John Cleare), p. 5 (Rob Matheson), pp. 26, 27 (David Simmonite), p.29 (Parkes).

Cover photograph reproduced with permission of Stock Shot/Nick Yates.

Our thanks to Andy McNae of the British Mountaineering Council for his comments in the preparation of this book.

Every effort has been made to contact copyright holders of any material reproduced in this book. Any omissions will be rectified in subsequent printings if notice is given to the Publisher.

Any words appearing in the text in bold, **like this**, are explained in the Glossary.

This book aims to cover all the essential techniques of this radical sport but it is important when learning a new sport to get expert tuition and to follow any manufacturers' instructions.

# CONTENTS

# INTRODUCTION

## Why do we climb?

The desire to climb is a strong human urge. Most of us start to climb from an early age. You may have climbed on furniture at home, up a tree or on a climbing frame in the garden. Or you may have climbed something higher: a wall in the park, or a small **crag** in the countryside. The sport of rock climbing developed from the natural physical challenge to get to the top.

While there is excitement and satisfaction in climbing, there is also a darker side. Falling off can lead to injury, even death. If you choose to take up the sport, this danger will not go away. Even when you come to use a rope it will still be there. However, part of the appeal of rock climbing is in learning how to recognize and cope with the danger.

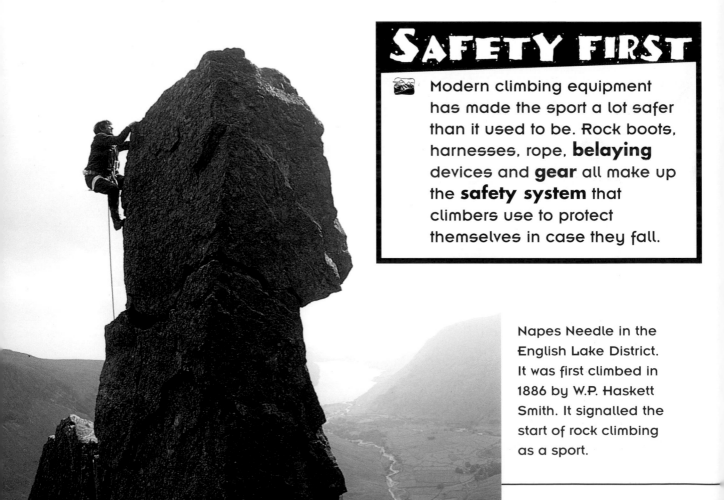

## SAFETY FIRST

Modern climbing equipment has made the sport a lot safer than it used to be. Rock boots, harnesses, rope, **belaying** devices and **gear** all make up the **safety system** that climbers use to protect themselves in case they fall.

Napes Needle in the English Lake District. It was first climbed in 1886 by W.P. Haskett Smith. It signalled the start of rock climbing as a sport.

## A brief history

Tradition has it that the sport of rock climbing started in Britain in June 1886, when W. P. Haskett Smith climbed a large spire of rock called Napes Needle, in the Lake District. He did this for no other reason than pure physical pleasure. People had climbed to the tops of mountains for thousands of years, by easy or by hard routes. But what Haskett Smith had done was different. He climbed a very difficult rock which did not get him to the top of a mountain. He was doing it simply to see if he could.

This climber is falling off a very hard climb. The ropes and protection will stop him hitting the ground. Ideally he would be wearing a helmet.

## Modern developments

Today, people all over the world enjoy the thrill of this unique sport. Climbs are done on sea-cliffs, crags found by roadsides or high in the mountains, and on indoor climbing walls. Indoor walls can now be found in most cities and many towns around the world.

# TYPES OF CLIMBING

## Indoor climbing

Today, there are indoor climbing walls close to where most people live. This is why most of us start at climbing walls. They have become very popular over the last ten years, with some schools, universities, and sports centres building their own. But the best tend to be at dedicated climbing-wall centres, which have qualified instructors. They are really climbing gyms, and are used by beginners, for improving climbing technique, or simply when the weather outside is poor.

Your local indoor wall is a great place to start climbing. There will be routes to suit all abilities, from easy to extremely hard.

## Climbing outside

For most, but not all, climbers, this is where it's at! The thrill of climbing on real rock somewhere in the countryside, with all the extra challenges of the weather and other unknown factors cannot be matched by an indoor climbing wall. You can buy guidebooks that describe all the climbs on all the **crags** in every climbing spot in a country. You will need considerable know-how, climbing equipment, some idea of what grade you climb at, and a partner.

# CLIMBING GRADES

 Climbing grades go from the easiest to the hardest. There are different systems in use around the world. The table below describes these grades and compares them approximately with each other.

| Britain | USA | Australia | France | UIAA* |
|---|---|---|---|---|
| Difficult | 5.3 | 11 | 2 | II |
| Very difficult | 5.4 | 12 | 3 | III |
| Severe (4a)** | 5.5 | 12/13 | 4 | IV/IV+ |
| Hard severe (4b) | 5.6 | 13/14 | 5 | V− |
| Very severe (4c) | 5.7 | 15 | 5/5+ | V |
| Hard, very severe (5a) | 5.8/9 | 16/17 | 5+ | VI− |
| Extreme 1 (5b) | 5.10a/b | 18/19 | 6a/6a+ | VI/VI+ |
| Extreme 2 (5c) | 5.10c/d | 20/21 | 6b/6b+ | VII−/VII |
| Extreme 3 (6a) | 5.11a/b/c | 22/23/24 | 6c/6c+/7a | VII+/VIII− |

\* Union Internationale des Association de Alpinistes.

\*\* The British technical grade is given in brackets. This shows how hard the hardest move on a climb will be.

 The grades in all countries are open-ended. They will continue to go up as long as people climb harder climbs. At present the hardest climbs in Britain are given the E10 grade.

Sea-cliff climbing in North Wales. The noise of the waves below and the exposure will make for a memorable experience.

# GEARING UP

Gearing up is the expression climbers use when they are getting ready to climb. They put on their rock boots, harness and helmet and get the rope and other special equipment ready. Don't forget to check all your equipment thoroughly before you start to climb and when you have finished.

## Helmet

Helmets protect the head and should be worn all the time when climbing outside. Many indoor climbing walls will insist on you wearing them as well. They protect you from hurting your head should you fall, as well as from falling stones.

## The rope

This is made from special nylon threads that are very strong and light. They are woven together and held inside a protective outer **sheath**. Most ropes are 50 metres long. They come in different widths, ranging from about 8.5 to 11 millimetres.

belay device

screwgate kabariner

## The harness

This is a waist belt connected to leg loops. It is made from very strong woven nylon. The rope is tied to the front of the harness when climbing. There are also special **gear loops** which make it easy for you to carry your climbing gear. It is very important that you read the manufacturer's instructions or get expert advice when learning how to put the harness on.

## Rock boots

These are special footwear with sticky rubber soles. They help you to stay on the smallest of footholds by creating lots of **friction**. They are very tight-fitting, which helps you to feel the footholds.

## Chalk bag ·····································▶

This is a small bag that holds your chalk and is attached to your waist by a **karabiner** or belt. Chalk helps to remove sweat from your hands when you are climbing hard or in a hot place. If your hands get too sweaty, you will slip off your handholds. So remember – when the going gets tough, chalk up!

## Clothes

There are two schools of thought – there are those who prefer tight-fitting clothes and those who like to hang loose. Take your pick! But remember, you need to be able to move easily and reach high with your arms and legs. Also bear in mind that indoor climbing walls will generally be warm, but outside on the **crags** you may be even hotter, or freezing cold. Take plenty of layers and consider taking a windproof or waterproof jacket just in case!

····· figure-of-eight descender

screwgate karabiners

## Karabiners ·····························

Karabiners come in various forms – **screwgate**, snaplink and pear-shaped. Make sure that you use the right one for the job.

# TOP TIP

 When it comes to clothes, lots of thin layers are more useful than one or two very thick items. Layers enable you to adjust your temperature easily and accurately to suit whatever climate you find yourself in.

# TRAINING FOR ROCK CLIMBING

## Warming up

Climbing is a sport and to get the best out of it, you have to train. One of the most important parts of a training programme is what you do at the beginning and the end of a session. You should always warm up. This means raising the level of your heart rate, to pump blood around your body, into your muscles and **tendons**. Do this by cycling to the wall or the **crag**.

## Stretching

Once you are warmed up, stretch your muscles and tendons. For climbing, you should concentrate on the shoulders, arms, elbows and fingers. Develop a routine that you go through each time. You should also do some light stretches at the end of a hard climbing session.

*Warm up*

Run or jog on the spot for 10 minutes.

*Shoulder stretch*

Bend each arm behind your head and hold for 30 seconds.

*Side bends* ··▸

Bring your hand up over your head as you bend to the side. Hold this position for 10 seconds. Repeat this six times, then do the other side.

## Strength and stamina

When you climb a route you will need strength and power to cope with short, very hard sections of a route. You will also need stamina to help you climb long routes. You can improve strength and stamina in special **bouldering** sessions. However, you must be careful not to over do these training sessions, especially when trying to work on your strength and power. You could end up with an injury, so remember to rest between climbs.

Stamina building requires you to climb on long, easy routes. This may mean **traversing** at low level, or doing a circuit or several circuits of the climbing wall. The important thing is to develop the ability to keep going, even when you feel tired or a little **pumped**.

Strength and power training comes through doing repetitions of short hard moves. Try doing the same move five times, resting for a minute between each attempt. Once you have mastered the move and can do it easily, find another, harder move to do.

# THE BENEFITS

 If you warm up and stretch before starting to climb, you will be less likely to strain a muscle or tendon. You will also find that you climb better and for longer. And if you cool down and stretch at the end of a session, you are less likely to be sore the next day.

# NUTRITION

 Climbers, like other sports people, need the type of food that gives them lots of energy. This means **carbohydrates**. Make sure that you eat plenty of these, and that you refuel after a hard session, and drink plenty of liquids. If you have been sweating a lot, **isotonic** drinks are the best for replacing lost salts and **rehydrating** your body quickly.

# THE SAFETY SYSTEM

## What the rope is for

The rope is there to help save a climber in the event of a fall. It is designed to withstand very large forces from falling climbers. It is also designed to stretch in order to absorb the energy created when a climber falls. The stretchy line used in bungy jumping works in a similar way – it stops the jumper from hitting the ground while the stretch prevents the person from being hurt by the force of the fall.

## Tying on to the rope

All climbers tie the rope to their harness. The best way to do this is using the **figure-of-eight knot**. Climbing is usually done in pairs, so one climber is tied on to one end of the rope and their partner is tied on to the other end.

How to tie a figure-of-eight knot.
········································►

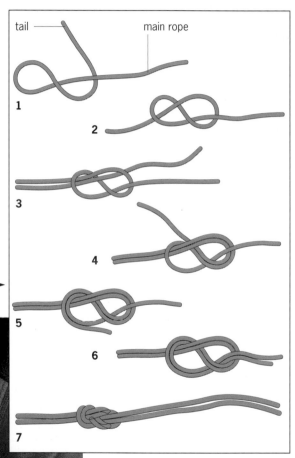

tail — main rope

1
2
3
4
5
6
7

This is a figure-of-eight and stopper knot, which all climbers must learn to tie. It has been tied into the climber's harness.

## Learning to belay

**Belaying** means holding and looking after the rope of the person climbing and being ready to stop them should they fall. You must always get expert tuition when you first learn to belay. There are no short cuts to learning how to do it properly. Remember, the life of the person who is climbing is in the hands of the belayer!

The climber (standing on the left) is ready to start the route, but should not leave the ground until the belayer has said they can start to climb.

As the climber gets higher, the belayer takes in the slack rope. Should the climber fall off, they will be held on the rope by the belayer.

## SAFETY FIRST

 Always check that you have put your harness on properly, tied your figure-of-eight knot correctly, and are using the belay device safely. If in any doubt, ask someone with experience to check everything for you.

# CLIMBING TECHNIQUE

## Staying in balance

Climbing is all about balance. It is important that you learn how to stay in balance, no matter what route you are on. Try to keep your weight over your feet. Don't get too close to the rock, but keep as much distance between it and your body as possible. This will also help you spot good foot- and handholds.

## Using your feet

Trusting your feet is one of the most important things to learn to do when you start climbing. It is the basis of your climbing technique. Your feet and legs are much stronger than your hands and arms, so you should learn to use them.

This climber is staying in balance by using both walls for her feet and hands.

## TOP TIP!

 Practise not using your hands at all on a **slab** that has a gentle angle. This will force you to concentrate on your feet alone and help develop your balance.

## Body position

Try not to climb like a robot! Change your body position to help you keep good balance as you move. Sometimes you may need to face the rock straight on, but sometimes you may need to turn your body sideways. Experiment with different ways of making the same sequence of moves. The more you do this, the greater the variety of moves you will have to help you overcome the most demanding of **cruxes**.

## Three points of contact

Try to maintain three points of contact with the rock. This may mean two feet and one hand while you move your other hand to find a new hold; or two hands and one foot while you move your other foot.

## Using small movements

Small movements are less tiring for your muscles. They also help to keep you in control of balance and body position. When you reach up high with your hands or feet, your body is put under greater strain. Get used to using smaller holds which are closer, rather than stretching for that large handhold that is almost out of reach!

## Use your eyes and brain

Scan the rock ahead and try to work out how you will climb it before you launch yourself. Do this from the ground before you start a route, but also as you climb.

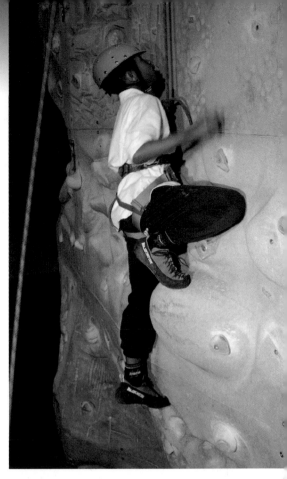

When learning climbing technique, it is a good idea to aim for 3 points of contact. This climber is moving his right hand up for a higher handhold, his other hand and both feet being secure and his body in balance.

## TOP TIP!

 Try going up one of your favourite easy routes, never moving your hands higher than your shoulders and never moving your feet higher than your knee position. Can you feel the difference as you climb?

# MOVEMENT ON ROCK

There are lots of special words that climbers use to describe particular types of movement on rock or types of holds. Here are just a few of the more common ones. When you go to the climbing wall or to a **crag**, think about the way you are climbing, and see if you are using any of these techniques.

## Jugs, crimps and slopers

These are all types of holds that you will come across. You will need to learn the different ways of using each hold to get the best out of them.

A crimp is a small handhold – you need to bend your fingers to use a crimp properly.

A jug is a large handhold which you can usually get your whole hand around.

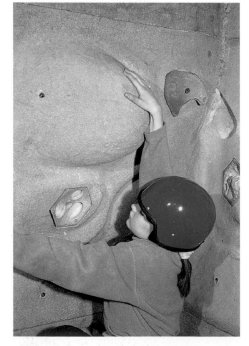

A sloper is a hold that is difficult to grasp but can be used by placing the whole hand flat upon it and applying pressure.

## Mantleshelving

You use this technique to get on a wall or ledge when you can get your hands on top but have no handholds to pull on. You have to push your arms over and get your weight above them. This can be very strenuous. Once you have done this, you have to get one leg onto the top of the wall alongside your arms, and then push yourself up until you can stand completely on top of the wall.

## Laybacking

This is a special technique that has been developed to deal with large cracks going up a corner of a rock face where there are few, if any, hand- or footholds. Placing both hands in the crack and your feet against the wall, you push away with your body, moving one hand and one foot at a time. Your arms may be almost straight. It is a very tiring technique, but if nothing else works, you will have to use it!

This climber is using a **heel-hook**. She has lifted her right leg onto a hold and will take some of her weight on this when she moves up. It is a very gymnastic technique!

## Edging and smearing

These words refer to types of footholds. Edging describes the use of the inside or outside edge of your rock boots on small holds. Smearing means getting a grip by using the **friction** between your rock boot's rubber sole and the rock face.

Edging with the inside of the right foot and the outside of the left foot. This allows the climber to have their body at an angle to the climb, which will help with balance and movement.

Now that you have an idea of what some of the **gear** is for and you have learned a little about climbing technique, you are ready to take the next step and put this information into action. The best way to go about this is to go along to your local climbing wall. Here you will find a friendly atmosphere and like-minded climbers. There will be climbs of all grades, from easy, through to middle ground, and on to climbs that are just about as hard as they can get!

## Bouldering

**Bouldering** means climbing without all the clutter of ropes and harnesses. Indoor walls are a great place to do this. There is usually a dedicated bouldering area, complete with crashmat to cushion your fall. As you are climbing without a rope you will hit the ground when you come off, so a mat is essential!

Make easy moves when you start bouldering. This helps to warm up your body and avoid injury through strain. Don't go too high. **Traverse** rather than go straight up. Bouldering is a great way to practise your technique and to experiment with different moves. You will learn even more by watching your friends climb.

## SAFETY FIRST

Try jumping off a few times in a controlled way. By doing this you will lose your fear of falling.

Bouldering at the climbing wall – no ropes, no harness, just a great amount of fun!

## Using the rope

The time will come when you want to go much higher than is safe for bouldering. At this point you must reach for a rope and harness, and find yourself an experienced **belayer**. Again, an indoor climbing wall is a very good place to start. Most walls will have ropes that are already in place on routes for all grades. All you have to do is put your harness on and tie yourself onto one end, while your belayer ties his or herself to the other.

If no rope is in place, someone will have to **lead** the route. Leading is the most exciting aspect of the sport. It is also the most dangerous. The leader has to climb the chosen route, putting **protection** into the rock as they ascend or clipping bolts already there. If he or she falls, it can be a long way. The height of the fall will depend on how far above the last bit of protection the leader was.

As belayer you are responsible for the person who is climbing. You must pay full attention to what he or she is doing.

This climber is clipping a bolt to protect themselves as they lead a route at the climbing wall. When you start to lead, always choose a climb well within your capabilities. Leading can be scary!

# CLIMBING HARDER ROCK

## Staying on steep rock

As you become stronger and more confident, you will want to climb more difficult rock. This often means getting onto steep or even overhanging ground. You may be outside or at your local wall. You may be **bouldering**, **leading** or going **second** on a route. Whatever the situation, work on your climbing technique to help save precious energy.

You must think of your feet all the time! Even on steep rock you must use your feet as much as possible. Keep in balance. Don't be tempted to reach too high for that big hold that's just out of reach. You will almost certainly fall off. Be content with any small holds that you can reach.

This climber has made a traverse and is about to climb a small overhang. Strength, experience, good judgement and a cool nerve are all needed on big, hard climbs.

## Rest when you can

Get into the habit of resting when possible. This may mean hanging off a straight arm, which is less tiring than hanging off a bent one. Or it may mean getting into a **bridging** position. Try not to think of your route as something that you must climb from bottom to top all in one go, especially if it's a long route. Divide it up with rest points where you can regain some energy and look ahead at the next set of moves.

## Coping with overhangs

Overhangs look very scary, but don't be put off attempting them. They will be strenuous, so don't try one as the first route of your climbing session. Make sure you are warmed up and ready to go. Remember to keep your feet on the rock, stay in balance, and use techniques such as the **heel-hook** where you can. Pulling yourself over the overhang can be the hardest move of all.

The bridging position. This climber is ascending a corner, and has positioned herself so that she can keep her balance well over her feet, which are kept on opposite walls.

# FALLING OFF

 At some stage you're bound to fall off. If you are bouldering, try to control your fall and stay relaxed. A tense body is more likely to be injured. Remember to roll over as you land. Don't land straight-legged. The commonest injury at a climbing wall is to the lower leg – ankles can easily get broken, so watch out!

 If you fall off while seconding a route, there should be no problem, you should fall only half a metre or so. If you are leading, it is a different matter, but still try to relax into the fall. The rope will stretch to absorb the energy. You just have to make sure you avoid any holds that are sticking out and stop yourself from slapping against the wall.

# LEARNING TO ABSEIL

**Abseiling** is the technique of sliding down a rope in a controlled way. It is used to come down from the top of a climb if there is no way to walk off. It is also used as a quick way of coming down from some **crags** when you need the time to do lots of different routes.

## Devices

The most common abseil device is called a **figure-of-eight descender**. It is a piece of metal with two holes. The rope is passed through one hole (usually the bigger of the two) and taken around the stem. The descender is then attached to your harness using a **screwgate karabiner** which is then locked shut. Abseil devices use **friction** to slow you as you slide down the rope.

Abseiling in extreme circumstances! This climber is coming back down after a long climb up a very high mountain.

# WATCH OUT:

 Make sure that all loose clothing and hair are kept away from the abseil device. If anything gets trapped you will stop.

 If you are not sure whether the end of the rope reaches the ground, tie a knot in it. This will stop you from abseiling off the rope.

 Don't bounce down or go at high speed. Either puts a lot of strain on the **anchor**. It also means that the device gets very hot due to increased friction, and heat damages the rope.

 Keep your fingers away from the device. Your controlling hand should be kept by your hip.

## Getting into position

You abseil backwards down the rope, with the rope hanging on one side of you. The important part of the rope is the part that has already passed through your abseil device. This is the controlling rope which you use to increase or decrease the amount of friction.

The hardest part of any abseil is starting off. Stand with your back to where you are going to begin your descent. Place your feet wide apart for greater stability, and lean back on to the rope, keeping yourself safe by holding onto the controlling rope. The first few times you do this make sure there is a safety rope attached to you. If you have one of these and let go, you won't fall to the ground.

Good position and the comfort of a back-up rope. This young abseiler is ready to take her first steps into the unknown – backwards!

## Descending the rope

Once you have leant back, and all your weight is on the rope, the fun begins! You can slowly let rope pass through your abseil device so that you start to descend. Keep your feet wide apart and your body at about 45 degrees to the rock. This will stop you falling forwards. But don't lean too far back, or you may turn upside down!

 **DANGER**

Abseiling is dangerous – many good and experienced climbers have been killed doing it. It is important to learn how to do it correctly and to check your equipment thoroughly every time you plan to abseil.

# THE GREAT OUTDOORS

## Where to go

Today, there are guide books to climbing outdoors for just about every region on earth. They will tell you everything you need to know. Most regions have **crags** that are known to be good for beginners. It is a good idea to head for them first. The grades will be easier, the **belays** generally good, and you will mix with other people at your level. Aim for somewhere close to a road, rather than one of the more isolated climbing regions – if something goes wrong it will be easier to get help.

## Outdoor factors

- If the rock is wet forget it and go somewhere else. Wet rock is harder to climb and not much fun!
- Holds can break off! You need lots of experience to deal with loose or dodgy rock.
- You won't find the holds picked out in convenient colours like at a climbing wall. You will have to learn to 'read' the rock. This means being able to see holds or guess where they might be, and what type they are, and how you can best use them. This takes a lot of skill and experience.
- The atmosphere will be different. It will be scarier, more exciting and more memorable.
- Don't forget to take in the views.

These climbers are using the guidebook to find their route. It is worth stopping before you get too close to the crag, so that you get a wider view of the rock.

## Coping with weather

Remember to take lots of different layers when climbing outside. In summer in the sunshine you may only need shorts, a t-shirt and some sunscreen. But if the wind gets up and the clouds roll in, you'll need a few warm layers and a windproof top to stop you getting cold.

Belaying outside on a cold day. This climber is keeping warm wearing a duvet jacket and gloves. Don't forget to take them off when you start to climb!

# DIFFERENT TYPES OF ROCK

 Granite is a volcanic rock. It is generally very good to climb on, being strong with good, positive holds.

 Limestone tends to be steep, with lots of little pockets for your hands and feet. You should treat this rock with care – it can be loose.

 Gritstone is known for its fantastic **friction**. This is because it is rough, like sandpaper. The holds are often rounded and hard to use, and there are cracks which can be very tiring.

 Sandstone is a softer rock. It is great to climb on. It can be **friable**, so should be climbed on with care.

# COMPETITION CLIMBING

Indoor climbing has developed around the world into a very organized activity. One of the most enjoyable sides to this has been the growth of competitions. These range from local **bouldering** leagues, to regional, national and World Championships.

## How competitions work

Most competitions have a junior and senior level, and are divided into male and female competitors. There are bouldering championships and there are **leading** championships. Some competitions last a day, but others might last over many different events which take place at different climbing walls. The points are added up until the final event is run. Then the overall winners in the different categories (junior, senior, male, female) will be known and announced.

Bouldering competitions are great fun! You will be tested against a series of increasingly hard short problems.

## Local competitions

If you are interested in taking part in a competition, contact your local climbing wall for details. They should be able to tell you about any events that they run, or of any events in your area.

You can also contact climbing clubs or the representative climbing organization, such as the British Mountaineering Council (BMC), which should be able to help you. The BMC runs a special junior climbers section called 'Gripped' which will have details on events, as well as much more to do with climbing (such as safety issues, courses, and so on).

## International competitions

These are held on a yearly basis. They involve the best climbers from all over the world. Lots of different events are held in different countries, where all the climbers go to compete.

This climber is taking part in a leading competition. Once again, the routes will start off easy (everything's relative!) and get harder ... and harder.

# CLIMBING AROUND THE WORLD

Climbing is a truly international sport. Many countries now have important outdoor and indoor climbing venues.

## The American scene

Yosemite National Park in California is known all over the world as one of the finest places to climb on high granite spires, such as El Capitan. Equally famous are Joshua Tree, also in California, and Smith Rocks in Oregon. Boulder, Colerado, offers excellent sport in the foothills of the Rockies, and on the other side of the USA, there is the Shawnagunk Ridge in New York State (known to climbers as 'the Gunks'!). These are just a few of the great places to go in this huge country.

Climbing in Yosemite National Park, California, USA. This is one of the world's most famous climbing venues.

## European heights

The European Alps are famous all over the world. They offer some of the best high-altitude climbing. Europe also has thousands of lower level climbing venues, the main type of rock being limestone. France is the most popular country, with climbing to be found in Brittany, the Mont Blanc Massif, Fontainebleau (just south of Paris), the Vercors, Gorge du Verdon, and the Mediterranean coast, to name but a very few places.

## British rock

Britain has one of the longest traditions of rock climbing. Although only a small country, with a limited amount of places to go, it nonetheless has some excellent **crags** and sea cliffs. These include coastal cliffs at Swanage, Portland, Cornwall, and Pembroke, Southern sandstone, and inland crags in the Peak District, Wye Valley, Yorkshire and Northumberland. High mountain climbs can be found in North Wales, the Lake District and in the Highlands of Scotland.

## Australia

In spite of being the flattest continent on earth, Australia has routes that attract people from all over the world. The Arapiles Tooan State Park is said by some to be the best rock climbing playground there is! It is in the State of Victoria, and consists of several miles of rock faces that are the delight of climbers. It also has a climate that allows all-year-round climbing.

Hard routes and hot sun – climbing at Mount Arapiles in Australia. This is a Mecca for climbers from all over the world. They come for the unique experience of climbing in this fantastic setting.

# GLOSSARY

**abseil** to lower yourself down the rope in a controlled way, using friction to slow you down

**anchor** the place on the rock face, mountain or indoor wall that you attach yourself to

**belaying** a way of holding a climber's ropes so that you (the belayer) can hold the climber if they fall

**bouldering** climbing without using ropes or harnesses. This is usually done at a climbing wall where there are spongy mats to cushion a fall

**bridging** a climbing technique that involves pressing the feet against opposite walls to keep balanced

**carbohydrates** complex sugars that the body needs to supply it with energy. Bread, pasta, rice and potatoes all contain carbohydrates

**crag** a small cliff used for climbing

**crux** the most difficult move or series of moves on a climb

**figure-of-eight descender** the device most often used for abseiling

**figure-of-eight knot** the knot most people use to tie the rope into their harness

**friable** rock that crumbles easily

**friction** a force generated when two surfaces rub against each other

**gear** the special equipment climbers use to protect themselves

**gear loops** the loops found on the harness where karabiners holding the gear can be kept

**heel-hook** the technique of putting one foot higher than your arms and hooking the heel on a hold, to help overcome an overhanging piece of rock

**isotonic** drinks that are absorbed into the bloodstream very quickly. They are used by sportspeople to replace fluid quickly when training very hard

**karabiner** a special strong metal clip used to attach the rope to an anchor or harness

**leading** to go up a route first, that is being at the sharp and risky end of the rope!

**protection** special gear used by leaders to protect themselves as they climb a route

**pumped** when a climber has been working so hard that veins stick out from their arms and their muscles have gone hard

**rehydrate** drinking fluid after sweating a lot

**safety system** the equipment that helps protect climbers should they fall off a route rope, includes the harness, karabiners, and belay devices

**screwgate karabiner** a special karabiner that can be locked shut

**second** to go second (seconding a route) is to climb after the leader as his or her belayer

**sheath** the tough outside of a rope which helps protect it from getting damaged

**slab** a rock face that has a reasonably gentle angle. Most beginners start to climb on slabs

**tendons** special tissue found in the body that connects bones to muscles

**traverse** climb sideways instead of upwards

# USEFUL ADDRESSES

Australian Sport Climbing Federation Inc
PO Box 431
Box Hill 3128
Australia
03 9894 7894
e-mail: hardrock@ozemail.com.au

British Mountaineering Council
177-179 Burton Road
Manchester
M20 2BB
0161 445 4747
e-mail: office@thebmc.co.uk

Mountaineering Council of Scotland
4a St Catherine's Road
Perth
PH1 5SE
01738 638 227

Mountaineering Council of Ireland
c/o AFAS
House of Sport
Longmile Road
Walkinstown
Dublin 12
00 353 1 450 9845

# FURTHER READING

*The Handbook of Climbing,*
Allen Fyffe and Iain Peter
Pelham Books

*Climbing Knots,*
British Mountaineering Council

*Safety on Mountains,*
British Mountaineering Council

*Ropes,*
British Mountaineering Council

*Climbing Wall Directory,*
British Mountaineering Council

*Climbing Rock* (video and booklet),
British Mountaineering Council

*Rockclimbing Essentials,*
Malcolm Creasey,
Anness Publishing

## Magazines

*High,* Greenshires Publishing

*Climber,* Myatt McFarlane plc

*On the Edge,* Greenshires Publishing

*Rock,* Wild Publications Pty,. Ltd

## Websites

www.rock.com.au

www.rocklist.com

www.craglink.com